You and Your Pet
Puppy

Jean Coppendale

First published in the UK in 2004 by
QED Publishing
A Quarto Group Company
226 City Road
London, EC1V 2TT

www.qed-publishing.co.uk

A Catalogue record for this book is available from the British Library.

ISBN 1 84538 284 6

Written by Jean Coppendale
Consultant Michaela Miller
Designed by Susi Martin
Editor Gill Munton
All photographs by Jane Burton except
Page 5 (top), Steve Grubman, Getty Images
With many thanks to Daniel and Shona Mackenzie
Picture of Sandy on page 29 by Georgie Meek
Creative Director Louise Morley
Editorial Manager Jean Coppendale

Printed and bound in China

Words in **bold** are
explained on page 32.

Contents

Your first puppy

► **King Charles spaniel puppies**

A puppy is a great pet. You can play together and have lots of fun. But puppies are not toys. They can be easily hurt, and they should be treated very gently.

When you play with your puppy, don't be rough – if you hurt it your puppy may bite. Remember you can't throw your puppy away if you get bored with it.

▲ A Labrador puppy

◄ A Boxer puppy

► A Husky puppy

Puppies are very cute – but puppies grow up into dogs. Most dogs like to play, but a fully grown dog may not be as cute and playful as a puppy.

Which puppy?

Puppies are all different. Some have long hair and some have short hair; some are small and some are big.

▲ **Small dogs like this Cairn terrier can be very active and may bark a lot.**

Puppies are different shapes and sizes

◀ **Dalmatian puppies grow into big dogs.**

▶ **Bull Mastif puppies will need a lot of exercise.**

A puppy should be at least eight weeks old before it leaves the litter and its mother.

▲ **Dogs with long hair like this Pomeranian will need a lot of brushing.**

Parent Points

When choosing a puppy, go to a breeder or rescue home. Seeing the puppy with its mother will give you the best idea of its eventual size. Avoid pet shops and dealers. Ask your local vet for advice.

If you are getting a rescue dog, the carers at the centre can help you to choose one with the right temperament and background to live with a child.

Look for a bright and active puppy that has a clean, shiny coat, clear eyes, a clean bottom and a moist, cold nose.

Lots of dogs

These dogs are all **pedigree breeds**.

▲ **West Highland terrier**

▶ **Collie**

◀ **Afghan hound**

◀ **Chihuahua**

▼ **Boxer**

◀ **Cocker spaniel**

▲ **Hungarian puli**

▲ **Dachshund**

9

Getting ready

Make sure that your home is safe for the puppy. Puppies enjoy chewing electrical wires, so make sure that these are all safely tucked away.

You should also always put your toys away somewhere safe when you have finished with them. If you leave toys lying around, your puppy might think they are toys for it to play with. Your puppy could swallow them and choke.

▲ **Make sure that there are no wires to bite and chew.**

Your puppy's tail will wag a lot, and may knock things over. Make sure that any breakable objects are well out of reach!

▲ Your puppy will race around and bang into things, so make sure that plants and ornaments are not too close to the edges of tables.

Parent Points

Never leave a puppy alone in a room. Puppies will instinctively chew anything they can get hold of – make sure that shoes, bags and any other chewable objects are well out of reach.

Check that there aren't any poisonous plants in the house or the garden – ask your local vet or garden centre for advice if you're unsure.

puppy shopping list

Your puppy will need:

◀ Two bowls, one for food and one for water – these should stand on newspaper or on a feeding mat

▶ A special spoon or fork – always use this to serve your puppy its food

▼ A brush

▲ A sleeping basket – or put a soft blanket or an old jumper in a box

◀ A carrying basket for trips to the vet and for other trips until it has had its vaccinations

◀ Toys for your puppy to play with.

▲ Rubber bones and other chewy toys will help to keep your puppy's teeth strong and healthy

Buy some toys and some treats for your puppy

▲ Puppy treats

▼ A collar with your puppy's name and address on it, and a lead

Saying hello

When your puppy arrives, take it out into the garden to go to the toilet. Do not chase it or grab it. Stay with your puppy and talk to it, so that it gets used to your voice.

Sit next to your puppy and stroke it along its side, from its shoulders towards the tail. Do not stroke or pat your puppy's head.

▶ **Show your puppy where its bed is.**

▲ **Your puppy will need something to eat.**

Show your puppy where its food bowl is. Your puppy should always have fresh, clean water to drink in another bowl near its food.

Parent Points

Puppies need correct training, handling and gentle guidance as soon as they arrive at a new home. This is to avoid bad habits and behavioural problems in the future. Training is an adult's responsibility but the family should work as a team.

Never leave a child alone with a puppy or dog.

Handle with care

Never hit your puppy, pull its ears or tail, or throw things at it. If your puppy gets scared, it may **growl** and show its teeth. Don't go near it, but quietly back away and leave it to calm down.

▲ **Stroke your puppy very gently.**

Only pick up your puppy if you are sitting down or kneeling, otherwise you may drop it. To pick it up, put one arm around its chest and the other hand under its bottom. Don't let its legs dangle down, and never pick it up by putting your arm round its middle.

◀ **Don't squeeze your puppy.**

16

▲ **Puppies need lots of sleep.**

If your puppy is sleeping, don't wake it up. Don't scare it by making loud noises near it.

Parent Points

Make sure your child doesn't tease the puppy, especially by offering it food and then taking it away. This may cause the puppy to jump up and bite at the food — and at the child. Never feed your pet from the table, and never feed it chocolate. Chocolate is poisonous to dogs.

Looking after your puppy

Once it is trained (see page 24), take your puppy for a walk at least twice a day. If your puppy gets very wet, when you get home, dry it with an old towel. If it has been walking in mud, rub your puppy with an old cloth, and brush off any dried mud. Wipe your puppy's paws gently with a towel or cloth.

Never tease your puppy with food.

▲ **Give your puppy special dog chews to keep its teeth strong.**

▶ **Be gentle when you brush your puppy. Do not hold it tightly or pinch it.**

Brush your puppy at least once a week. Always start at the shoulders and brush down towards the tail. Be gentle. Do not touch its head. If your puppy starts to **growl**, stop, and move away into another room.

Parent Points

Never give a puppy small or cooked bones, especially chicken bones, as they may make it choke. Try giving it chews that look like bones or sterilized marrow bones from pet shops.

The puppy should not leave the house until it has had all its vaccinations.

Never leave a puppy or dog in a car on a warm day, even if the windows are open, as dogs overheat very quickly.

You: puppy's life cycle

▼ A female dog can have puppies when she is between six months and one year old.

5

▶ At 10 to 18 months, a puppy is fully grown.

4

◀ **At two weeks old, a puppy cannot see.**

▶ **At three to four weeks old, a puppy will start being weaned from its mother's milk.**

◀ **At eight weeks old a puppy should visit the vet for its first vaccination.**

Let's play!

Have a tug-o-war with your puppy, using an old piece of soft cloth or a special puppy toy.

▼ **Give your puppy a special toy.**

A puppy may bite playfully if it gets very excited. Don't hit it, or shout – just stop playing, and leave the room.

Make sure that your puppy has some toys to play with when it is alone, so that it doesn't get bored.

▲ **Play ball with your puppy. Make sure the ball is not too big, too small or too heavy.**

Parent Points
Always supervise your child and the puppy when they are playing together. When they play indoors, make sure that all tables and chairs are moved out of the way to avoid accidents. The puppy should be trained never to bite even when playing, as this could lead to more aggressive behaviour as the dog gets older.

Training your puppy

Teach your puppy its name. Sit or kneel in front of your puppy. Quietly say its name over and over again. When it comes to you, praise your puppy and stroke it.

Do not let your puppy jump up on the furniture when you are playing. Never shout at or hit your puppy, even when it is naughty. When your puppy is good, give it lots of praise.

Try not to let your puppy jump up at you. Sit or kneel down to stroke your puppy. Do not put your face too close to it.

Your puppy should always wear a collar with a name disc, or your vet can give it an **identity chip**.

When you take your puppy for a walk, hold on tightly to its lead. Always go out with an adult. Make sure your puppy's lead and collar are not too tight.

▲ **Your puppy will love going for walks.**

puppy watching

▲ Puppies pant when they are hot and thirsty. It helps them to cool down.

◀ When a puppy comes towards you with its tail in the air, it is pleased to see you.

► When a puppy crouches down and wags its tail, it wants to play.

▼ If a puppy shows you its teeth or growls, keep away and do not touch it.

saying goodbye

Your puppy is growing and getting older all the time – just as you are.

Many older dogs have stiff joints, and they may become ill. If this happens to your pet, keep it warm and make sure that it gets plenty of sleep. Stroke it gently and talk to it quietly.

Sandy last summer

◀ **As it gets older, your dog will need shorter walks, and it will sleep more.**

My dog Sandy

Keep a special scrapbook about your pet

If your pet is very old or ill, it may die. Try not to be too sad, but remember all the fun you had together.

You may want to bury your pet in the garden. Plant a special tree or bush or some flowers where it is buried.

puppy checklist

Read this list and think
about all the points.

✔ **Puppies
are not toys.**

✔ **Dogs
can live
for up to
18 years
- will you
get bored
with your
pet?**

✔ **Your pet will
love you very much
for as long as it lives.**

✔ **Don't carry your
puppy about unless
it is an emergency.**

✔ **Treat your
puppy gently -
as you would
like to be
treated
yourself.**

✔ **Puppies
have feelings,
just as you do.**

✔ **How will you treat
your puppy if it
makes you angry?**

✔ **Why do you
think a puppy
may bite?**

Parents' checklist

● **You**, not your child, are responsible for the care of the puppy.

● Dogs can be very expensive to keep. Consider the following before you commit yourself to buying a puppy:
- vet's bills (seek advice from your local vet)
- food bills
- kennel bills when you are away
- possible training fees – some puppies may need to attend obedience classes.

● If you are out of the house for more than 3–4 hours a day, a dog is not a suitable pet.

● Do not keep even a small dog in cramped conditions.

● Are you willing to walk a dog twice a day? It is a legal requirement to collect up any mess your dog makes.

● Do you have any other pets? Will they get on with a dog?

● Always supervise pets and children.

● If you want to buy a pedigree dog, do some research first.

● All dogs need vaccinations, worming and flea treatments. Neutering is advised for all male and female dogs. Ask your vet for advice.

puppy words

A puppy or dog can **bark** and **growl**.

A puppy's **nails** can be very sharp.

A puppy's fur is called a **coat**.

A puppy's feet are called **paws**.

A **breed** is a special type of dog, such as an Alsatian or a poodle.

Pedigree breeds are special types of dogs that have been bred over a long time to have certain features and colours.

A **vaccination** is an injection of medicine to prevent a puppy from getting ill.

A puppy is **weaned** when it gradually stops feeding on its mother's milk and is introduced to other foods.

Your vet can insert an **identity chip** under your puppy's skin with your pet's details on it. Vets and animal centres can 'read' the chip with scanners so that lost animals can be returned home.

Index